KW-339-797

# CONTENTS

*For Stewart, with love*

Poetry Library
102807
COPY NO. 2

# WHITE FISH WITH PAINTED NAILS

Jill Dawson

WITHDRAWN FROM THE POETRY LIBRARY

POETRY LIBRARY
SOUTH BANK CENTRE
ROYAL FESTIVAL HALL
LONDON
SE1 8XX

slowdancer

**Jill Dawson** was born in 1962 in Durham and grew up in West Yorkshire. She was the major Eric Gregory Award winner for 1992 and has twice been a writer-in-residence, as a young writer of 25 in Doncaster and, more recently, at Fareham College, Hampshire. She is the editor of two books for teenagers and *The Virago Book of Wicked Verse* and *The Virago Book of Love Letters*; she is currently compiling another anthology.

*White Fish with Painted Nails* is her first collection.

Acknowledgements are due to the editors and publishers of the following, in which some of these poems first appeared: *Ambit*, *Envoi*, *The Eric Gregory Anthology*, *The Independent*, *Slow Dancer* and *Writing Women*.

"The Crossing" has been published in *Virago New Poets*, *The Virago Book of Birth Poetry* and *In the Gold of Flesh*.

Cover Illustration by Melvyn Nutbeam.

Published by **Slow Dancer Press**
59 Parliament Hill
London NW3 2TB

Copyright © Jill Dawson

ISBN 1 871033 26 8

# THE COUNTRY

## THE LOG CABIN

hastily constructed
by a biker's moll, name of Esther
or Evelyn, no one can remember.
They still call it Pike Peasely's Old Place,
and the men come visiting some nights,
to sit around the rusty oil barrel
we use as a stove and tell me how
Pike got busted for growing weed.
And how his old lady whooped his ass.
Then they forget about Esther
or Evelyn and ask questions like
why didn't he strip the bark offa the logs?
or fill in the gaps between em?
or *insulate* the place? and sooner or later
one of them exclaims:
you sure as hell have *light* coming in!
Then they start up
about the parties they used to have
when old Pike was around,
and I listen and nod,
until I can hear their cowboy boots
stamping on our deck;
smell the beer and sweat and sweetherb tobacco,
and I long to be an Esther or an Evelyn,
with big capable hands
and someone's rough beard in my blouse;
sneak out behind the outhouse in moonlight,
swing my ponytail
and unbuckle some jeans ...

## HEARTBEAT

Here on the mountain at night
I go to sleep
feeling the black sky touch my face,
feeling the stars on my tongue.
I hear my baby sigh in his sleep
I hear my heart beat
I hear my lover breathing.

Lying in his arms
I am in the dark hollow of a dug-out boat
cold is the water
cold the screams
of a circling hawk.

THE POETRY LIBRARY

## DRIVING

The washboard took someone off the road.
One two three and it was done:
like skimming stones, but off the mountain
instead of the sea. I pass the spot
on my maiden drive, glance fearfully
at the car, sideways in a ditch of sage-brush
and skunk's cabbage.
You can skid on this dust
easy as apple pie. Hit the smallest rock
and wham — careering over the honey-grass hills
like a kicked stone.

But I am not alone. You eye the ditched car too,
and your small voice
pipes out instructions. You're doing fine.
Mind this next bend. Slow down.
In the mirror all I see is dust,
beneath us the hills strung out like rows of washing;
sheets, towels, small green vests.
You're driving, mum! you yell, amazed.
I'm driving.

## MOUNT CRAZY

Patrick
beats up on his old lady. Tells me:
she's a lil blonde perty thing;
beat him first with the frying pan.
Can you believe that?

Kay
drinks my coffee, pulls a beer can
from her pocket. Tells me:
everyone up on this here mountain
is an alcoholic.
Don't you know that?

They called their youngest kids
Patrick and Patricia.
He don't see nothin' funny in that.
He sticks James Dean on bare log walls
four kids and them in a one room shack.

When I ask the name of the road
up the mountain that leads to their cabin,
Patrick says: Oh that?
I call that
"My drive."

The one time I see them together
they're around their woodstove
quiet as pie. Tell me:
saw a mink, white as a ghost,
2,000 bucks walk right in here,
cool as you like.
Can you believe that?

## AT SUMMIT LAKE

Not to stand on the side
fully dressed
and look,
but to be in it, in it!
Braving leeches
and garter snakes
and cold slimy weeds
for this:
longing
to be level with the violet tails
that cling to the reeds
like tiny blue flags,
to feel the cool surface
of the water
closing
around me,
to see, at nose level,
a single
dipping bird.

## SUMMIT LAKE REVISITED

I'm swimming in a cat's eye marble,
all colours and light
in this ball dropped
in the lap of the mountain.
Cobalt blue above,
glass edges blurred with green.

First the green of the lily roots,
melting into bull rushes
and further, the green of the Lodgepole pine,
yellow at the core.
The arms and hands are mine,
parting the water:
green and jet the rich, thick surface
closing behind me.
The only sound
my          splash.

When a cold patch
washes my legs
I suddenly know
what depths I'm in.
At any moment the slither of a garter snake
will circle my ankle;
a deadly lily root drag me under.

I'm swimming frog-style
away from the violet tail
about to fly in my face,
sending me into choking panic.
Or that chicken hawk overhead,
deciding to swoop
not at that silver flash of fish,
but at me:     my yellow skin!     my green hair!

When I stumble out,
dripping, shivering, laughing,
I've no idea what I feel.
Triumphant? Elated? Relieved?
Or disappointed?
To have come so close to the summit
but not reached it,
      again

THE POETRY LIBRARY

## THE LION'S DEN

Downtown in the Laundromat
waiting for twenty pairs of shorts
in small medium and large
to become the grey that passes for clean
I need some change
for the washing machine
venture next door into The Lion's Den
hoping there's no one there I know
but at the counter is a guy called Bo
head sunk in his giant mane
like something out of ZZ Top
if you know what I mean

Rumour has it he fancies me
so I stop in my tracks
fumble over my request for quarters
but too late — he's heard the accent
looks up    drawls Did I hear somewhere
you got you a truck to sell?

In the semi dark he and the barmaid
are only two sets of teeth
I take a breath    step back
nervously say we have a Fort GMC
with a Chevy engine
pronouncing the 'ch' as in *cherry*
He shrinks back into his corner
I make my escape
saved by the insult
        to an American institution

## SLEEPY COUGAR FOUND NAPPING IN PINE CREEK TREE

*Tonasket. A wayward cougar*
*didn't seem the least bit curious ...*

... What **were** we doing that day
only seven miles away? Probably I was
sunbathing naked with the ants
on a scratchy rug, you were busy
chopping wood, not the least bit curious

that several people, a number of dogs
and a cat were milling around the tree
with only the slow pendulum
of its tail to give it away

I was busy fantasising your death
this time a quick axe
to the back of the head
you were not the least bit curious ...

*He asked Geoff what's with the dummy?*
*Geoff said the heck it is, the tail's moving*

Or maybe I had a letter that morning
one to soothe me, from the inner city,
maybe I was cheering you with news
of Blackburn Rovers, at any rate

I was doing something, that's for sure -
so were you, so was everyone

the morning a wayward cougar wandered along
to a concrete contractor's backyard
only a few miles away
from where our three-year old
tried to play with his new bike
which couldn't handle the rocky terrain
and threw him off once again

*John and Jim, two wildlife agents*
*were called in to remove the animal*
*from the tree, first drugging it* while
you and me continued our sultry scrapping

the axe poised in mid-air
sap bursting from a chunk of Ponderosa
A tractor with a front loader
was needed to pick up the sleepy body

The wild cat was released
at an undisclosed location
No one seemed           the least bit curious

## THAT NIGHT, DRIVING HOME UP THE MOUNTAIN FROM OROVILLE

Someone staggering home
  lurching in our spotlight
  on all fours, their fat
backside swaying under the
  shadowy Douglas firs.
I yell   stop the car
jump out, excited,
spill the flashlight everywhere:
  Lodgepole. Tamarack. Gravel. Stones.
Ponderosa pine cones.

But nothing moves
  to your obvious relief,
quick to start the engine again,
  slam the door.
I say   there was no danger
  it was only a hoary marmot
  a bear     a giant porcupine
Nothing like the things
  we meet at night
on our way home in Hackney

THE POETRY LIBRARY

## SWIMMING AT OSOYOOS LAKE

The water so cold, I'm scalding.
Every pore is singing.
Steam rising from the place
in the water where a gull circles
a strange fish with white skin
and painted nails.
The Canada geese fly over
making messages
but in another language.
I'm alone out here.
Swimming over the border
of two countries.
A tiny plane lands
between the Tameracks
and the Ponderosa Pines.
Behind that mountain
is my home. The first time
I've ever called it that.
And those others, that man and child,
blue and shaky? That's love,
too far to swim to,
that's another country.

# THE CITY

## THE CROSSING

All night the sea tossed me
like egg yolk in a basin
and rocked the baby in my belly

So here, arriving,
it is not I, but we
all churned up and frothing
and still, at the window,
the sea of our crossing.

Milky, simmering,
she laps at our door
while I'm lying in water,
drowning, distraught

Even in the bath
I'm assailed by kicks
the vicious struggle
of an ugly chick

I lie fearful at night
while wind, rain and sea
puncture the fine membrane of the house

and the child inside
rolls like an eyeball
beneath skin grown fine as an eyelid

## LOVE POEM FOR A NEW BABY

With your fish mouth
madly sucking
you strip me of poetry,
lie like a pebble
green-furred and ancient
at the bottom of every dream.

Frogs leap
and I never hear them,
worship only
your small hot mouth
your light furled hand
that falls like a petal
on my breast
while you sleep.

Named for an island
and all the islands
I never visited.
Lewis,
daily

you take me there

## THE BAD MOTHER

screaming in the street
shaking
  her small boy by his skinny arms,

and all because
he wouldn't put on his shoes
and made them late
and she can't afford a taxi

every day some small cruelty
she can never undo,
and never forgives herself for;
hoarding them up
like lost babyteeth, kept in a drawer.

she says:
if only I could be
three again, struggling with my shoe laces;
start all over, go back to the beginning

shake my mother

abuse my father

## THE BLACK EYE

Lid slumped — a soft blue plum,
petal from an over-bloomed tulip.

Every day I watch her eye beneath
a billowing sail, unfold
its story; changing from lilac
to shrieking violet. In the playground,
running, she is a tiny one-eyed pirate. The mother
a stout short woman in her tough wool coat

says, once, hanging her daughter's coat
on a knee-level peg, I'd like to
catch her by that bloody scarf and hang
her out the window.

We hold meetings about this statement.
Too bald even for us to miss. At risk.

Carefully, my job is to copy this
into her file. Details of her injuries.
That eye has started opening
again, unfurling like a rosebud, a fist.
I note that luckily it seems there is
no permanent damage to the iris.

## STING-RAY

Sting-Ray he thought was a winged submarine
from the TV programme   not this
giant flopping mushroom curling
at the skin of the water while he
sneaks his hand into the tank
to stroke its fluted underbelly.
She watches her small son
out-staring an omelette
which eyeballs him back from two slit eyes.

The dolphins at Marine World
have been delivered back into the wild.
Sorry Madam   it's cruel
and unfashionable to keep them.
He will have to content himself
with the butter-chinned sharks skimming over
his head in the glass-roofed corridor.
And he does try even ducks a little
as rows of tiny teeth comb the glass
glide away   vacant   disinterested.

The day out. Distraction but he can't help
remembering, and though she struggles, droning:
Sand Dollar   Red Sea Cucumber   Green Sea Urchin
Sharp-Nosed Crab   Dunce Cap Limpet
Black Turban Snail —
he still asks, interjects:
Is Dad coming back then?
and even the Red Velvet Spider Crab can't do it.
The assistant, wet sleeves,
probes under a well-lit, green-slimed rock
produces one for him
holds it professionally by the claws, offers its
red velvet back for him to touch
— it won't hurt you love —

He drops his hand. Turns away.
The adults wave and snap after him, open and close
their mouths.   Sharp pincers.   Lies.

## THE DEVIL

I was hungry
He fed me
fish and okra
and rice with coconut

I was thirsty
He gave me Guinness
and bade me drink

I was lonely
He laid me down
but I had not come
for that

I had come
to hear him speak
and so he did

He said
when you know what it is
you want
you will get it
(For Jah tell we that)
Meanwhile
don't rush
you are young still
Eat your okra
is good for you
... and stay awhile ...

It was dark and rainy
      late Sunday
and steamy in his kitchen

We had not seen each other
in some time

Lord I was tempted
to do as he begged me
run away with him
abandon
      everything

## NIGHTLIFE

I dreamed his heat again last night
and woke up tasting guilt,
lying beside you, anticipating blows.

We have an agreement. Only in dreams
will I ever sneak
into that wet black lycra again
red marks between my eyes
from wearing the goggles too tight;
the blue and the splash and the spearmint
and the smell of sperm and chlorine mixed.
The pool, the hot tub,
   my first jacuzzi.
Bubbling in places
I'd never bubbled before.

The lifeguard was silent, smooth
and inviting.
It was always up to me.
You misunderstood, you thought he forced it.
I can hardly blame you
for wanting to think the best of me.
But think the worst.
Believe the worst, imagine it
in all its glory, red and black, slip and slap,
in the deep, deep south,
the white man's worst nightmare:
to think, she wanted it.

## TRAVELLING

She loves to ask men about their conquests.
Tell me again about the kissogram
that dressed as a mermaid,
that Dutch biker
you bent across your Harley
on that tour of Crete,
and the student nurse, the one you
smuggled into the Embassy party
so she could straddle you, up against
the tiger-skins and stag-horns
and all the other trophies.

Tell me, she says, the exact
size and feel of their breasts ...
The up-turned bellies of sparrows?
Didn't Leonard Cohen say that?
Melons, that's more like it, don't try to be
original. Pendulous, pert, provocative ...
She sighs, disturbed, caught between
titillation and envy; what it must be like
to travel the world,
as men do, sampling.

Eighteen. Her first trip to the States.
Alone, on a white-hot Florida beach,
trying to lie on a cool square of towel,
the young man who told her she had the body of a
movie star

and then jumped on it, punched her,
pummelled her into the beach

## THE APPLIANCE OF SCIENCE

Since he left
she's taken to washing under her arms
at the kitchen sink, no longer the strict
border between kitchen and bathroom.
She's unpicked at the seams
spilling over

After she's dropped the kids
she crawls back to bed
with a pile of magazines
and a Cadbury's Cream egg,
leaves the washing-up festering
only gets up
to straddle the Zanussi
in its final spin

The kids have started to worry about her.
The youngest thinks she's developing
agoraphobia, the eldest calls her a slut.
She answers the door to the postman
in a cotton-lycra nightie, so short
and flighty, she has to hold it at the thighs.

Nobody thinks to touch her.

## THE LUTHIER

Dusting, she finds a jar of gold globules;
the rabbit glue he used to stink the flat with.
And behind that — other jars, pickled memories.
Tripoli. Dragon's blood. Benzoin. Mastic.

The index finger he once borrowed,
tying a knot in a skein of horse's hair
combed across his knee.
She remembers how he bubbled and toiled
while she hoovered outside compulsively.

Why did he leave
the Gam Boge. Sandrac. Sweet smelling Elemi?
Did he mean to torture her with them
along with the lemon-wood tailpiece
his home-made purfling cutter
and his tape of the Sensuous Baroque?

Now she will never know
if it was all a lie
or whether he really did come close
to discovering what he called
the Greatest Secret of All.
Stradivari's recipe for violin varnish.